THE
BUG BOOK

BY DR. HUGH DANKS

Illustrated by Joe Weissmann

A Somerville House

HAMLYN

D0226703

This edition first published in Great Britain 1988
by
The Hamlyn Publishing Group Limited,
Michelin House, 81 Fulham Road, London SW3 6RB
Reprinted 1988, 1989
Produced by Somerville House Books Limited, Toronto, Canada
First published by Workman Publishing Company, Inc., New York, U.S.A.
Copyright © 1987 by Somerville House Books Limited
Illustrations © 1987 by Joe Weissmann
Copyright this edition © 1988 The Hamlyn Publishing Group Limited
ISBN 0 600 55935 1
Printed in Hong Kong

*The publishers would like to acknowledge the assistance given by
The Natural History Museum of London, The National Museum of Natural
Sciences, Ottawa, and The Royal Ontario Museum, Toronto.*

This book is also supported by WATCH, the young people's conservation club. Why not join the network of WATCH clubs around the country, many of which go on "bug watching safaris"! Write to WATCH for membership details and receive a free bumblebee poster by mentioning the Bug Book. WATCH, 22 The Green, Nettleham, LINCOLN LN2 2NR.

Contents

Bugs, Bugs, Bugs

Bugs are fun, and The Bug Bottle lets you discover that for yourself. Use it to catch many of the bugs that live near you, then turn it into a hotel for your new guests. The Bug Book tells you how to keep some kinds of bugs for a short time, how to handle them, and what to look for. Create your own projects and give your guests different things to do.

Bugs are also amazing. Discover how the whirligig beetle got its name, how the praying mantis snares its food and how the grasshopper sings. Capture a caterpillar and watch one of the most miraculous changes in nature: right in your bottle, a slow-moving, wormlike creature may transform itself into a graceful flying butterfly or moth.

Bugs are important, too. Although some kinds harm crops and trees or eat clothing and carpets, most bugs are useful. They help to keep the soil healthy for growing plants, and they provide food for many birds and fish.

Begin today! Take your bottle and book

outside, and start looking for bugs. Catch them. Observe them. Be amazed. And, most of all, have fun.

What Is a Bug?

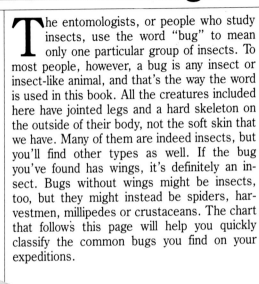

The entomologists, or people who study insects, use the word "bug" to mean only one particular group of insects. To most people, however, a bug is any insect or insect-like animal, and that's the way the word is used in this book. All the creatures included here have jointed legs and a hard skeleton on the outside of their body, not the soft skin that we have. Many of them are indeed insects, but you'll find other types as well. If the bug you've found has wings, it's definitely an insect. Bugs without wings might be insects, too, but they might instead be spiders, harvestmen, millipedes or crustaceans. The chart that follows this page will help you quickly classify the common bugs you find on your expeditions.

GROUP:	INSECTS	SPIDERS	
Examples:			
Body Parts:	3	2	
Pairs of Legs:	3	4	
Antennae:	1 pair	None, but 1 pair of pedipalps (feelers)	
Notes:	Many adult insects fly. All insects go through a process of change, from eggs to larvae to adults, called metamorphosis. (For more information, see pages 26–27.)	Most spiders spin silk. Many of them use the silk to weave webs for catching prey.	

HARVESTMEN	MILLIPEDES & CENTIPEDES	CRUSTACEANS
2	Always more than 15	Usually 14
4	At least 15, often more	Usually 7
None, but 1 pair of pedipalps (feelers)	1 pair	2 pairs, sometimes hard to see
The legs of harvestmen are longer and thinner than those of spiders.	These creatures are always long and slender and have many legs.	Most crustaceans, such as crabs and lobsters, live in water; only a few live on land.

*Caterpillar pretending
to be a twig*

Several caterpillars are master disguise artists. When they're not busy eating, or when danger is near, they keep absolutely still and pretend to be twigs.

Some beetles, for their size, are much stronger than we are. They can lift more than 300 times their own weight—or the same as a man lifting 20 cars!

If a flea were as big as a man, it could easily jump over a skyscraper!

Honeybees have to visit over 250,000 flowers to make a pound of honey.

There are more kinds of insects in the world than there are every other sort of animal put together!

Glow worm (male)

The wingless female glow worm has a special organ on the underside of her body that produces light. On warm summer evenings you can see it glowing to attract the winged male glow worms.

Different kinds of glow worms in other countries can make bright flashes of light, and they are sometimes called fireflies or lightning bugs.

The larva of the glow worm eats snails!

Catch a glow worm in your bottle. It may continue to glow there. Look at it in the light, and discover a little, soft-bodied brown beetle!

Bug & Bottle Tips

1 Keep still and look closely. Bugs are not always easy to see. Be patient and watch—this is how insects hunt, too.

2 If you have trouble finding bugs, spread some debris and water from a pond bottom, or some earth or dead leaves, onto a small, pale-coloured unbreakable tray. Shake the tray gently, and the bugs will move across it—making it easier for you to see and catch them.

3 Try to identify the sorts of bugs you find, using this book as a guide. If you can't find them here, look in a more comprehensive book such as the *Country Life Guide to the Countryside of Britain and Northern Europe* (Hamlyn) or *A Field Guide to the Insects of Britain and Western Europe* (Collins).

4 Catch a bug in your bottle. Some kinds of bugs will walk or fly up into the bottle if you place it over them; then you can slip the lid underneath. Other kinds will stay still on a leaf; in this case, place both leaf and bug inside the bottle.

Bug & Bottle Tips

Be alert to what's going on around you. Stay away from the road and other dangerous places. Ask an adult to help you catch the water bugs.

5 Be gentle. Compared to a bug, you're a giant. When you place a bug in the bottle or take one out, don't pinch it or pick it up by its wings. Instead, let it sit in your hand.

6 Make the bug feel at home. Create a miniature environment in the bottle by adding twigs, grasses, water or whatever else was in its surroundings. Any bug found feeding on a leaf should be given the same kind of leaf.

7 Keep the bottle away from direct sunlight. Heat can kill.

8 Use a magnifying glass for a closer look at the bug. Remove some of the twigs or grasses from the bottle. Put this material back when you're finished.

9 Bug Bottle Projects suggest activities that let you see the bugs in action. Try creating your own projects for the bugs.

10 Keep a list of the bugs you observe. Make notes about what you see them doing in your bottle.

11 Become an expert. Learn more about various bugs: check your local library for other bug books.

12 Put the bug back when you've finished observing it. (The bug may die if you keep it too long.) Try to put the bug back exactly where you found it.

Don't Touch!

Watch for this sign beside some of the bugs in the book.

Be sure not to touch bees, centipedes, wasps and other bugs that can bite or sting you.

Be sure not to touch insects like water boatmen—even though they might be harmless, they look similar to other kinds that can bite you.

Be sure not to touch butterflies and other fragile insects because you can easily hurt them.

Look on Leaves

Leaves anywhere and everywhere are good places to hunt for bugs because they give food and protection to many insects. Certain bugs are fussy eaters, so you'll find them on only one specific type of leaf; take away their choice of leaf, and they won't eat at all. Watch, too, for the insect-hunters that are searching the leaves to feed on the leaf-eaters—you can also collect these bugs in your bottle.

Leaf beetle

Leaf beetle

APPEARANCE: The leaf beetle has an oval or rounded body with short legs. The characteristic green or yellow colouring of several kinds of leaf beetles comes from certain substances in the plants they eat. Other kinds are shiny and metallic-looking.

FOOD: A variety of plants, depending on the age, stage and type of leaf beetle. In the larval stage, some types eat the roots and stems from the inside out; others prefer leaves. Adults can be found on the leaves of many plants. Look on oak leaves, willow trees and bramble bushes to find a few of the common leaf beetles.

NOTES: There are more than 24,000 kinds of leaf beetles in the world. Several of these beetles cause serious damage to crops. Some of the smaller ones can jump and are called "flea beetles." The females of certain kinds protect their eggs by covering them with a gluelike substance.

Leafhopper

Leafhopper

APPEARANCE: This particular type of leafhopper is easy to recognize by its bright colours. Other kinds are pale green and smaller in size, but they have the same long, narrow shape.

FOOD: Various grasses as well as wild and cultivated plants, bushes and trees, depending on the leafhopper species.

NOTES: The leafhopper has a sucking tube for feeding on plant juices. In many sap-sucking bugs these juices pass rapidly through the bug's body, and part of them ends up back on the leaves in the form of a sugary liquid called *honeydew,* which becomes food for ants and other insects. Leafhoppers also spread plant diseases by feeding first on a sick plant and then on a healthy one.

Ladybird

APPEARANCE: The ladybird is a small, rounded and usually brightly-coloured beetle. The telltale red or yellow colours combined with black markings keep birds and small mammals away by warning them that this bug tastes bad.

FOOD: Aphids, which are tiny bugs related to the leafhopper.

Ladybird larva and adult

BUG BOTTLE PROJECT

Look for ladybirds on the leaves and stems of plants. If you see any leaves covered with aphids, a ladybird is probably nearby. Gently place the bug in your bottle.

Ladybirds eat aphids. Because aphids weaken plants by sucking out the juices, gardeners welcome ladybirds and consider them good friends.

See if you can find the larva of the ladybird. It, too, eats aphids. Most ladybird larvae are elongate, warty black creatures with red or yellow spots. They're found on the same leaves as the adults, and you can keep them in your bottle as well.

Give the bug fresh aphids to eat each day that you keep it. The aphids themselves are easily crushed, so don't touch them; just place them in the bottle on their leaf or stem. The ladybird may eat several aphids, one after the other.

Like all beetles, the ladybird has hardened wing-cases that cover its transparent flying wings. When you're ready to let the ladybird go, take it outside and place it on your hand. Sooner or later you'll see it spread its flying wings, tucked under the coloured wing-cases, and fly away.

See how many types of ladybirds you can find—different kinds have different numbers of spots.

Shieldbug

Shieldbug

APPEARANCE: This common green shieldbug blends into its leafy background with great success. Like all shieldbugs, it has a body shaped like a shield. Look for other varieties with different colours.

FOOD: Various garden plants, including flowers and fruit as well as leaves.

NOTES: Shieldbugs are sometimes called stink bugs because they produce a strong-smelling substance to ward off birds and other enemies. This substance tastes terrible to us, as you already know ·if you've ever eaten a raspberry previously sat upon by a shieldbug. Like leafhoppers, shieldbugs feed on plant juices by means of a sucking tube.

Weevil

Weevil

APPEARANCE: Sometimes called a "snout beetle," the weevil has a long beak that helps it feed on plants. Its body is very hard, almost as though the bug is wearing a suit of armour.

FOOD: Weevils feed on all kinds of plant matter – buds, stems, fruits or leaves – according to the species.

NOTES: Although the adult weevil is tough and strong for its size, the larva is a blind, legless little grub that lives inside the leaf, bud, stem, fruit or seed of the host plant. Weevils make up one of the largest families of insects in the world, with over 60,000 different species.

Caterpillar

APPEARANCE: The caterpillar, which is the larva of a moth or butterfly, has many different forms. It can be fuzzy or smooth, bright-coloured or dull. Most kinds have several extra sets of short, round "legs" on their plump bodies to help them hang on to the plants upon which they feed.

FOOD: The leaves of plants, usually one or a few specific kinds depending on the type of caterpillar. When caterpillars become butterflies or moths, they usually feed on nectar from flowers.

Swallowtail caterpillar

BUG BOTTLE PROJECT

Look for caterpillars on leaves and twigs. When you see one, pick the leaf or twig that you found it on and place it in your bottle. Check your fieldguide first to make sure you don't take a rare species.

Do not handle hairy caterpillars—the hairs of several kinds can irritate your skin or eyes.

Each day, give the caterpillar freshly picked leaves from the same type of plant you found it on. Remove wilted leaves from the bottle.

Watch the caterpillar eat. Put your bottle in a cool place, and the caterpillar will eat slowly; in a warm place, it will eat much faster. Remember, too much heat can kill.

If you keep the caterpillar for a long time and feed it diligently, you'll notice the larva eating more and more the bigger it gets.

Partially line the bottle with a piece of stiff, non-slippery paper. If you're patient enough to feed the bug until it's fully grown, it will begin another stage in the process of *metamorphosis* by spinning a cocoon or a support for the pupa on the paper or on a twig of the food plant. Eventually, it will emerge as an adult butterfly or moth. You should let it go soon afterwards without touching its wings. Turn the page for more information on metamorphosis.

Metamorphosis

All insects assume different forms during their lifetime. This process of change, from egg to adulthood, is called metamorphosis.

The *eggs* of most insects are very small. They hatch into *larvae*, which usually look like grubs or caterpillars.

The larvae grow by eating until their skin is too tight. Off splits the old skin to reveal a new one underneath! The new, larger skin is soft and has to harden. Larvae change

Pupa shedding larval skin

Pupa

their skin, or *moult*, several times during this stage of their life.

The larvae of butterflies, bees, flies, beetles and many other insects eventually moult into resting *pupae*. Some larvae spin silken cases called cocoons, to protect them when they reach the pupal stage. Inside the pupae, insects change into very different creatures: the *adults*.

Newly emerged adult

After the adults emerge, they wait for their soft, new wings to harden before they can fly. Soon the females prepare to start the life cycle all over again. Usually they use the food stored in the larval stage for laying eggs. The females of many species lay hundreds and hundreds of eggs. The eggs hatch—and the cycle begins again.

Incomplete metamorphosis.

Except for their fully developed wings, some adult insects, like shieldbugs, grasshoppers and dragonflies, show much less change from the larval stage. There is no pupal stage in the life cycle of these bugs; instead, their adult wings grow gradually throughout the larval period.

Look in a Pond

Insects that live in water have special ways of swimming, breathing and obtaining food. Some bugs live in ponds all their lives. Others live underwater only during their larval stage, which usually lasts longer than the adult stage. When the adults emerge, they live outside the pond but come back to it to lay eggs. Look for pond bugs in many stages of development both above and below the water. You will need a net to catch some pond bugs. Others you can catch by scooping them up with your bug bottle.

Diving beetle

APPEARANCE: This beetle is big, streamlined and oval-shaped. It has long hind legs, which it moves together at the same time like oars as it swims rapidly through the water.

FOOD: Insects and soft-bodied creatures such as several kinds of worms, insect larvae and tadpoles.

NOTES: Like all typical insects, the diving beetle gets its air from tiny tubes, or *tracheae*, inside its body. This air is continuously renewed from an air bubble carried under its wings. Every so often, the diving beetle must get a fresh bubble by visiting the surface. Although it is a big beetle it readily flies from one pond to another.

Water boatman

APPEARANCE: The water boatman is streamlined for underwater swimming. Each of its flattened, hairy swimming legs is like the blade of an oar, "rowing" the boatman quickly through the water. The boatman looks similar to the backswimmer, a water bug that may bite you if you handle it.

FOOD: Small pond creatures.

NOTES: The water boatman carries air beneath its wings and also in special hairs on the underside of its body. This film of trapped air appears silvery. Like the diving beetle, the boatman must come to the surface at intervals to renew its air supply.

31

Caddis

APPEARANCE: Caddis, the larvae of caddisflies, look like tiny moving pieces of the pond bottom. They carry around miniature houses made of small pieces of leaves, twigs, shells or other items from their surroundings.

FOOD: Little plants or pieces of animal material. Some caddisflies feed occasionally on liquids such as flower nectar and the honeydew from insects.

Adult caddisfly

Caddis cases

Caddis

BUG BOTTLE PROJECT

Look into a clear pond until you see tiny piles of sticks or leaves that seem to move on their own.

Scoop some pond water into your bottle. Then gently pick up a caddis, in its case, with your fingers and quickly add it to the new environment you've created.

Look into the pond again. Is there another type of caddis to catch and add to your bottle?

Get a grown up to very gently pull some of the caddis' house apart *underwater*. Keep in mind that a caddis cannot breathe out of the water.

Look at the feathery hairs over the caddis' body. These hairs are gills that help the larva take in the oxygen dissolved in the water.

Give the caddis tiny pieces of whatever its first house was made of or even pieces of the house itself. Watch it build a new house.

Try giving the caddis a different set of building materials. It may not use the ones you supply, because most larvae build with only one type of material. However, someone once succeeded in getting a caddis to build a house of gold dust!

Whirligig beetle

Whirligig beetle

APPEARANCE: This insect is oval-shaped and usually black. It has extremely short antennae, long forelegs and short, paddle-like hind legs.

FOOD: Small insects, taken both on and below the surface of the water.

NOTES: Whirligig beetles were named for their habit of spinning crazily around in circles on the water's surface. Look for this activity near the water plants at the edge of a pond or quiet stream. The eye of the whirligig beetle is divided into an upper and lower part so that the insect can see above and below the water at the same time.

Pond skater

Pond skater

APPEARANCE: The pond skater is slender, with long, thin legs. The weight of the body is evenly spread out to keep the bug from sinking below the surface. Thus it runs easily on top of the water.

FOOD: Chiefly insects that fall onto the water's surface and cannot fly off again.

NOTES: Also known as "water skaters," pond skaters have tiny water-repellent hairs on their feet to keep them dry as they walk on the surface.

Dragonfly larva

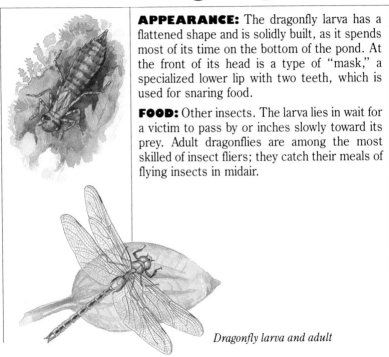

APPEARANCE: The dragonfly larva has a flattened shape and is solidly built, as it spends most of its time on the bottom of the pond. At the front of its head is a type of "mask," a specialized lower lip with two teeth, which is used for snaring food.

FOOD: Other insects. The larva lies in wait for a victim to pass by or inches slowly toward its prey. Adult dragonflies are among the most skilled of insect fliers; they catch their meals of flying insects in midair.

Dragonfly larva and adult

BUG BOTTLE PROJECT

Look for a dragonfly larva moving slowly on the bottom of a pond, marsh or boggy lake, near the edge.

Pick up the larva and gently place it in your bottle with a little pond water.

The larva is like a jet-propelled submarine. Touch it lightly with a small stick and watch it force water out of the back of its body and shoot forward.

Put in a stick that reaches almost to the lid of the bottle. If you're lucky enough to have a larva that's ready to change form, you'll see it climb up the stick and turn into an adult dragonfly. If so, do not touch its wings and let it go outside as soon as the wings have reached full size and hardened. See pages 26–27 for more information on this change.

If you keep the larva longer than a week, you will have to feed it. The dragonfly larva eats only living prey, so put a small water bug in the bottle. Watch quietly, and you may see the larva's "mask" in action.

Look on the Ground

Most bugs that live in or on the soil prefer damp places. Many hide under stones, logs or boards. Some use these places as daytime homes and come out only at night; others, like ants, are busy during the day and shelter at night. Lift up the shelters gently, and you'll see that certain bugs stay clinging to them while others scurry away or vanish down holes into the soil; still others curl up into motionless balls. Always put the shelters back in exactly the same place.

Wolf spider

Wolf spider

APPEARANCE: This spider is sturdy and mobile, unlike some of the more fragile spiders that sit on webs. Its dark colours help it hide easily in leaf debris or among sticks and rocks.

FOOD: Other bugs, which usually are captured at night. While other spiders trap their victims in webs, the wolf spider hunts like a wolf—searching over the ground for its prey and seizing it with powerful jaws.

NOTES: Like other spiders, the wolf spider spins silk from special little turrets, or spinnerets, at the back of its body. Instead of building a web, however, this spider uses its silk chiefly to make a bag that will protect its eggs. The eggs hatch after a few weeks, and the tiny new spiders are carried on the female's back for several days before setting out on their own.

Earwig

Earwig

APPEARANCE: The earwig is easily recognized by the pincers at the back of its body. The male earwig has stronger, more curved pincers than the female.

FOOD: Some fruits and flowers, the leaves of some plants, decaying material and other small insects.

NOTES: Earwigs were once thought to seek shelter in people's ears, but in fact they simply like to hide in damp little crevices—which is where you'll find them during the day. Unlike most other insects, they guard their eggs in shallow nests in the soil until hatching time. The pincers are used most commonly for defence or during mating, and also for helping to unfold the wings before flying.

Woodlouse

APPEARANCE: The woodlouse's shape, flattened from top to bottom, lets it squeeze under stones. This bug is a crustacean, not an insect, so it has seven pairs of legs instead of three pairs.

FOOD: Small, rotting pieces of plants.

Woodlouse

BOTTLE

BUG BOTTLE PROJECT

Look for a woodlouse by turning over stones in the woods or in a park or garden. If you can't find one this way, put out some flat stones; after a few days, one or two woodlice may have moved in beneath them.

Put some slightly damp leaf litter into your bottle with the woodlouse. This will provide both moisture and food.

Turn over the woodlouse and count its legs. You should see the seven pairs that are characteristic of most crustaceans. Woodlice are among the few land species of crustaceans; most other types, such as lobsters and crabs, live in the water.

If you find several woodlice, put them in the bottle together. Remove the leaf litter, then place a slightly damp piece of paper on one side of the bottle and a dry piece on the other. Make sure the two are well separated. You'll soon see that the bugs stay near the damp paper in the bottle, because without moisture they would dry out and die.

Try another experiment to find out whether woodlice prefer light or darkness. Put the bugs in a large, covered glass dish. Cover one end of the dish with a black cloth and leave the other end in the light. Where do the woodlice go?

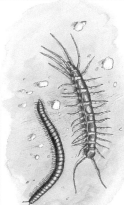

Millipede and Centipede

APPEARANCE: Some people confuse millipedes and centipedes, but the two are not really alike. Millipedes have a rounder body and shorter antennae than centipedes. They also have two pairs of legs on each segment of their body, whereas centipedes have only one pair per segment.

FOOD: Millipedes eat decaying plant material. In contrast, centipedes actively hunt and eat insects, subduing their prey with poison from their jaws; most kinds can poison only other bugs, not people.

NOTES: Millipedes and centipedes are not insects but belong in their own distinct groups of bugs. Millipedes will usually remain still or curl up when you expose them. Centipedes, which are much more active, will quickly run away.

Rove beetle

Rove beetle

APPEARANCE: The rove beetle is different from the ladybird and most other beetles in that it has distinctive short wing-cases that do not cover the whole body.

FOOD: Chiefly small insects and other soil-dwelling creatures. Most rove beetles use their sharp jaws to catch their prey, although others eat only dead animals or fungi.

NOTES: The rove beetle is an active runner even though it also flies well. Certain kinds run with the tips of their bodies lifted up. Because many kinds have glands there that produce repellent substances, some scientists believe that this action helps to put off predators.

Ground beetle

APPEARANCE: This beetle is easy to recognize by its long, thin antennae, strongly armoured body and long legs that allow it to run rapidly across the ground.

FOOD: Other insects. Some kinds of ground beetles even climb up plants at night to attack caterpillars, which they cut open with their powerful jaws.

Ground beetle

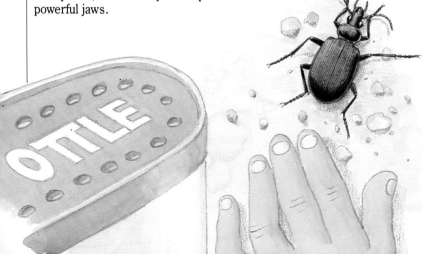

BUG BOTTLE PROJECT

Lift up stones, boards or logs until you see a ground beetle. Quickly put your bottle over the bug as it runs, then slip the lid underneath.

Turn the beetle over by tipping your bottle. Watch how its long legs are used in righting itself. The beetle may have difficulty if it cannot get a proper grip on the bottle.

Feed the ground beetle every few days. This bug is a nighttime hunter, so it's not likely to eat during the day. Give it a tiny piece of raw meat before you go to bed; in the morning, you'll be able to see where it's been feeding.

Use a magnifying glass for a close-up look at the long antennae of the ground beetle. The antennae are of a simple type, made up of many similar short segments. The insect uses them to feel and smell the world. When it eats, for instance, it will inspect its food with them.

Try catching ground beetles by setting your bug bottle (without lid) into a hole dug in the soil. Leave it overnight and in the morning check for bugs that may have fallen in.

When you let the ground beetle go, tip it out onto a smooth, level piece of ground. Watch how fast it runs away.

A Word About Ants . . .

Ants are among the most common insects found on the ground. There are several different types, but usually ants are black or red in colour. Many live in nests like little cities that they build by tunnelling underground or in rotten wood. All the ants in one nest or colony can be the children of a single big queen ant who spends her whole time laying eggs. During her lifetime, the queen in a large nest may lay over a million eggs!

The eggs laid by the queen hatch into grublike larvae. These larvae are fed by the adult worker ants. When fully grown, the larvae of many kinds make little silken bags called cocoons, often wrongly called "ants' eggs." Like caterpillars, the larvae change into pupae inside the cocoons. In a few weeks, adult ants emerge, ready for work.

One of the workers' major tasks in looking after the colony is to find food. Most ants eat almost anything but usually prefer sugary substances or dead and living insects. Some kinds protect aphids in order to take their honeydew, much as humans keep a herd of dairy cows. Other ants grow gardens of edible fungus inside their nests. Food of all types is stored in special rooms and can be carried to

Cross-section of a colony

...and More Ants

the queen and larvae as required.

Once a year, the colony produces special winged ants—both smaller males and bigger females—that come out of the nest and fly up into the sky. Some of them mate. Then the females settle, shed their wings and become queen ants, ready to found new colonies. The males soon die and never accompany the new founding queens. Look for these winged ants on the warmest and most humid summer days.

Find an ants' nest.

Put out baits and track the ants that come to them back to their nests. Certain ants are very fond of sweet things, so try placing a sugar cube on the ground. Or put out baits such as any dead insects you find or tiny pieces of cooked meat. Ants are incredibly strong—watch them lift pieces of food many times larger than themselves.

One worker ant repairs a tunnel...

. . . while another carries food to the colony

You can also discover an ant colony by looking under stones. Sooner or later, you're bound to find one. Only the upper tunnels of the nest will be visible.

Other colonies.

Ants are not the only insects that live in colonies. Termites are common in tropical areas; bees and wasps occur everywhere. Each colony has the same basic structure—one queen that lays eggs and many "workers" with specific jobs in the colony. Workers feed the queen, look after the eggs, larvae and pupae, repair tunnels, search for food and defend the nest against enemies. Some species have different types of workers that are specialized for their duties; for example, several kinds have extra-large, strong-jawed guards that fight attackers.

Look in a Field

Fields are full of insect activity, so they're good places for watching many different kinds of bugs. Flowers attract bees, butterflies, beetles and other insects with their lure of sweet nectar. Many bugs eat the abundant leaves, while others scurry over the ground. If you are on holiday in a warm country, you may be lucky enough to see a praying mantis waiting quietly for passing victims.

Cabbage white butterfly

Cabbage white butterfly

APPEARANCE: There are three kinds of white butterflies that feed on cabbages, but the large white, or cabbage white, is the biggest. The caterpillars are yellowish-green with black spots.

FOOD: The caterpillars feed on cabbages and related plants, and can do a lot of damage in gardens. The adult butterflies are attracted to garden plants like buddleia that produce lots of nectar.

NOTES: Although the caterpillars can be garden pests, many of them will never grow into adult butterflies because they are attacked by tiny wasps that lay eggs in them. The wasp larvae eat away the inside of the caterpillars' bodies and eventually kill them.

Praying mantis

Praying mantis

APPEARANCE: One of the largest field insects, the praying mantis is protected by a green or brownish colouring that lets it hide among leaves and grasses or against the ground.

FOOD: Many other kinds of insects. The mantis waits in ambush for other bugs to come too close, then strikes out with its spiny front legs. It always eats its prey live.

NOTES: The mantis is large and strong so that it can catch and chew its food. Unlike us, it can strike at flies faster than the flies can react by flying away! Of all the insects in the world, the mantis is the only one that can turn its head around to look behind itself. The praying mantis is found in southern Europe, Asia, America and Australia; it is an exciting insect to look for.

Harvestman

APPEARANCE: The harvestman looks something like a spider, and it gets its name because it was first seen in fields at harvest time. Its legs are much longer and thinner than the legs of most spiders. Comparatively speaking, if a man had legs as long as the harvestman's, he would stand 12 metres off the ground!

FOOD: Small live insects, dead insects and small pieces of decaying plants.

Harvestman

BUG BOTTLE PROJECT

Place your bottle in the harvestman's path and gently shoo it in.

Watch how this bug keeps its second pair of legs wide apart and off the ground. It moves them constantly while it walks and uses them as feelers, much the way insects use their antennae.

Touch the bottom of the bottle with a wet finger to place a tiny drop of water there. If its feelers find the drop, the bug may taste it with its mouth or drink it.

See how the bug cleans its legs by drawing each one slowly through its jaws.

Find the tiny eyes on either side of the black spot on the top of the bug.

Return the bug to the field after a couple of hours—otherwise it may dry up in your bottle. Gently tip the bottle onto the ground and let the bug walk out without damaging its long legs.

Longhorn beetle

Longhorn beetle

APPEARANCE: This beetle is named for its very long antennae. Some kinds have antennae over three times as long as their bodies. The insect shown here is just one type of longhorn beetle. Note its striking black-and-yellow colouring. Because it looks like a wasp it is not eaten by birds.

FOOD: Nectar and pollen from flowers are eaten by the adult longhorn beetle. Its larva eats the solid wood of dead and living tree trunks, making round tunnels in the process. The larvae of all longhorn beetles tunnel in wood.

NOTES: Many kinds of longhorn beetles attack trees, but usually when the trees are dead or dying. Some larvae of large longhorn beetles, known as "sawyers," make a buzzing noise in dead trees as they feed; you may be able to hear one "sawing" in a fallen log in the quiet woods on a warm summer day.

Bumblebee

Bumblebee

APPEARANCE: The bumblebee's yellow or red colouring combined with black warns predators to stay away. Bees sting! Their furry bodies help keep them warm and allow them to be active when it's too cool for other insects to fly.

FOOD: Nectar from flowers. Bumblebee larvae feed on honey made by the adult from nectar.

NOTES: Only the large queen bumblebees survive the winter. In spring, they come out of dormancy and start new nests in holes in the ground. Food for the colony is stored in little honey pots inside the nest. By summer, the colony normally contains the queen, many worker bees and, eventually, males and new queens. The colony then operates in a manner similar to that of an ant colony. See page 48 for more information.

Grasshopper

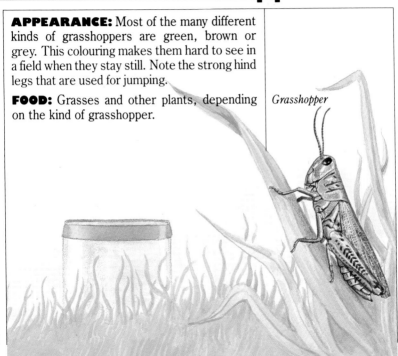

APPEARANCE: Most of the many different kinds of grasshoppers are green, brown or grey. This colouring makes them hard to see in a field when they stay still. Note the strong hind legs that are used for jumping.

FOOD: Grasses and other plants, depending on the kind of grasshopper.

Grasshopper

BUG BOTTLE PROJECT

Listen to the grasshoppers sing while they're in the field—they may not do so in your bottle. Many kinds sing by rubbing their wings and legs together. They sing best in warm sunshine.

When you see a grasshopper jump or fly through the air, watch where it lands. Stalk the insect, catch it in cupped hands and place it in your bottle. You'll find it easier to be a successful hunter on a cool, cloudy day, when grasshoppers are less active. Another way to catch a grasshopper is to gently lower your bug bottle over the insect – like in the picture on page 13.

Watch the grasshopper produce a black or brown liquid from its mouth when it's disturbed. This liquid won't hurt you, but it does irritate the small animals that prey upon the insect.

Experiment with several different types of grasses or other plants if your grasshopper is a fussy eater. Start with those that were around the grasshopper when you caught it. Watch how its jaws move from side to side when it eats, not up and down as ours do.

Place the grasshopper in a large empty box and watch it jump. For their size, grasshoppers can jump as far as a man leaping the length of two football fields!

61

Bugs That Look for You!

You won't need to search for some bugs. Instead, they'll come hunting for you! Female mosquitoes, black flies, horse flies and midges seek you out so they can take your blood, which they need in order to develop their eggs. Some kinds of

Did you know that flies land on you so they can drink your perspiration?

bugs, found mainly in the tropics, infect people with yellow fever, malaria and other dangerous diseases.

Mosquitoes can find you even at night, because they use their

antennae to home in on your smell and to detect the warmth and moisture of your body. Their mouths have thin needles that pierce your skin to draw out the blood.

Bug Terms

Adult Final stage in the metamorphosis of insects. An adult produces the next generation of eggs.

Antennae Feelers on the head of insects and their relatives, used for touching and smelling.

Beetle Member of the largest group of insects, noted for their hardened forewings.

Caterpillar Larva of a butterfly or moth.

Centipede Member of a group of bugs, differing from insects. For more information, see chart on pages 8–9.

Cocoon Silken case made by many insects to enclose and protect the pupa.

Colony Organized group of insects that live together.

Crustacean Member of a group of bugs, differing from insects. For more information, see chart on pages 8–9.

Dormancy Resting period during unfavourable conditions, as in winter.

Grub Larva of some kinds of insects.

Harvestman Member of a group of bugs, differing from insects. For more information, see chart on pages 8–9.

Honeydew A sugary substance deposited by aphids, leafhoppers and related insects after they feed on plants.

Insect Member of a group of bugs. For more information, see chart on pages 8–9.

Larva Young stage of many groups of insects, with a different form than that of the adult.

"Mask" Modified lower lip of dragonfly larva, used to catch food.

Metamorphosis Change in form, from egg to adult, that takes place in insects. See pages 26–27.

Millipede Member of a group of bugs, differing from insects. For more information, see chart on pages 8–9.

Moult To cast off an old skin, revealing a new one, so that growth can take place.

Nectar Sweet secretion of flowers, attractive to insects.

Pupa Resting stage between larval and adult stages in metamorphosis.

Spider Member of a group of bugs, differing from insects. For more information, see chart on pages 8–9.

Spinnerets Little turrets at the back of a spider's body, from which the silk is spun.

Tracheae Tiny tubes inside the bodies of insects that carry the air they breathe.

Wing-cases Hardened forewings of beetles, used to protect the flying hindwings.